PRIVATE VIEWS OF SNOWDONIA

Private Views
of
Snowdonia

PHOTOGRAPHS BY STEVE LEWIS L.R.P.S.

ESSAYS BY THE PEOPLE OF THE SNOWDONIA NATIONAL PARK

Published by Gomer Press
in association with The Snowdonia Society

First Impression 2005
Second Impression 2005

ISBN 1 84323 485 8 (Softback)
ISBN 1 84323 484 X (Hardback)

© photographs: Steve Lewis
© text: the contributors

This book is published with the financial support of the
Welsh Books Council.

Printed in Wales by Gomer Press, Llandysul, Ceredigion

WORCESTERSHIRE COUNTY COUNCIL	
495	
Bertrams	01.05.06
942.925	£19.99
KD	

Wherever possible in this book, place-names
within the Snowdonia National Park have
been standardized so as to be consistent with
*Rhestr o Enwau Lleoedd/A Gazetteer of
Welsh Place-names* (University of Wales Press)
to avoid confusions that may arise from local
variations, whether they be on signs or maps.

ACKNOWLEDGEMENTS

We are deeply indebted to the thirty contributors to this book for so willingly sharing their reflections and experiences of the Snowdonia National Park. Without them this book could not have been created. Bryn Terfel's willingness to write the Foreword is greatly appreciated. Morag McGrath took responsibility for liaising with contributors in relation to their articles, and, along with Rob Collister, shouldered the bulk of the editorial responsibility. However, inevitably Snowdonia Society staff were also involved at times and we thank Rob Owen, Dan James and Marika Fusser for their help. We also thank Annis Milner for her assistance with some of the Welsh translations.

We are most grateful to the staff at Gomer, particularly Ceri Wyn Jones, for their support and encouragement from the first day we discussed the project with them.

Steve Lewis and the Snowdonia Society

CONTENTS

FOREWORD BY

BRYN TERFEL

Photo: Nigel Hughes, Porthmadog

Landscape and people are inextricably linked. Snowdonia is not a wilderness area but has been lived and worked in for thousands of years. It is essentially a man-made landscape and one that is outstandingly beautiful. The National Park is the largest of the three Welsh Parks, extending from Conwy down to Aberdyfi in the south, and from Harlech across to Bala in the east. It encompasses a great diversity of landscapes, ranging from dramatic mountain peaks to tranquil valleys, superb lakes, fast-flowing streams and waterfalls, ancient forests, the heather-clad Rhinogydd of the south, beautiful river estuaries and the fine coastal area around Harlech. There are still areas where one can experience a sense of space, solitude and even silence.

Nearly all land in the National Park is privately owned. In this respect British National Parks differ from most other parts of the world. Yet what does ownership mean? Every contributor to this book feels and conveys a sense of ownership for his or her special place. The identifiable Welshness of the Snowdonia National Park makes it unique and this is reflected in many of the contributions, and in the fact that this book is being published in both English and Welsh.

It is a book that provides a perspective on Snowdonia rarely seen; that of the everyday people who live and work in the area, who have helped, and are still helping, to shape the area and its culture. We are privileged that they have chosen to share with us, in their own words, their thoughts, ideas, memories and emotions, and allowed us a small glimpse of what makes the Snowdonia landscape and its communities a very special part of the world.

INTRODUCTION

When Steve Lewis approached the Snowdonia Society with the suggestion that we should collaborate on a photographic book about the National Park, the idea was received enthusiastically. We knew the high quality of his work and the project he had in mind sounded an exciting one. Rather than focus solely on his own interpretation of the National Park landscape, his vision was to produce images reflecting the perspectives of people who lived and worked in the area.

The basic idea was simple: to ask a selection of local people to choose a favourite place or area in Snowdonia and to write about why it was important to them. Steve would then produce a photograph that sought to reflect the contributor's feelings about the location.

The initial problem was whom we should approach as potential contributors. Our main criteria for selection were that contributors live or work in the Snowdonia National Park (or be known to have a very strong association with it) and had made a significant contribution to the area. We endeavoured to include people from as diverse a range of age groups, occupations and locations as possible, but publishing constraints meant we had to restrict the number to thirty. The final choice is inevitably biased to people known to the Snowdonia Society, for which we make no excuses. (We did decide that no current member of the Society's Executive Committee or other photographers could be included!). While we were keen to include some well-known names because of their strong association with Snowdonia, we were also clear that this was not to be a record of 'the great and the good' only. Many of the contributors are probably unknown outside their local community.

Despite many never having written for publication before, all the contributors have produced thought-provoking works, which are rich in warmth, insight and imagination. Their words are a testament to their understanding of, and deep affection for, Snowdonia. In writing about their chosen site, some contributors have focused on the beauty of the landscape, others reflected on their early memories or specific experiences of the area. Many have a strong sense of the history of their site, an awareness of the way previous generations have left their mark on the present-day landscape.

The perspective of local people, presented in their own words, and interpreted by a photographer with extensive knowledge of the area, provides a refreshing and intimate insight into the Snowdonia National Park. It provides a unique and lasting record of this beautiful part of the world.

MORAG MCGRATH
(Snowdonia Society)

Private Views of Snowdonia

CRIB GOCH

Crib Goch is about four-hundred-and-fifty million years old. It is a great lump of volcanic rock made up of mica, quartz and felspar and it is the last of these three that gives it a pinkish aspect. Crib Goch crouches above Nant Peris and has fascinated me most of my life as a painter.

I have painted it from every side but usually from deep down in the valley of Nant Peris, from where I can see its ridge with the tower-like lump of rock at the western end of it. It appears to preside over the valley and the lesser crags of Clogwyn y Person and Gyrn Las. Waterfalls pour down to join the river below and one of these that flows through Cwm Glas I have painted many times.

As the sun swings from East to West behind the ridge, it leaves the mountain a dark and often forbidding shape, for it is only as the sun begins to go down that the light touches a part of the mountain and then its western flank becomes bathed in a golden glow.

I love Crib Goch when it is covered in snow and the sky is bright behind it; for then the snow becomes darker than the sky and, in a perverse way, becomes more intriguing to an artist.

There are foxes and polecats on the lower slopes of the mountain and once I saw a stoat, bright in its winter ermine, among a pile of rocks above the river. There are herds of feral goats in the crags around Nant Peris, but seldom have I seen them on the sides of Crib Goch itself. Lower down the valley there is a herd in Cwm Eilin, but usually I see them in cliffs further up on the lower slopes of Glyder Fawr and Glyder Fach. Ravens and peregrines nest below Crib Goch, there are dippers on the river and lower down I was lucky enough once to see a pair of ring ouzel.

In the past many painters have worked around Crib Goch. Turner painted on the mountain as did Cornelius Varley, while most of the nineteenth-century artists included it in their paintings of Eryri. They only came in the summertime so they never saw the snow on the mountain. I am lucky because I can see and paint Crib Goch through all the seasons of the year, in the summer sun and when the winter storms rage around the cockscomb ridge and even when the driving rain brings mystery to the land.

SIR KYFFIN WILLIAMS

Winter solstice sunrise, Crib Goch.

THE MIGNEINT

Whenever I have a day to escape the hurly-burly of work, I drive northwards to the Migneint, the wild piece of land that lies between Bala and Betws-y-coed. Or at least people think that it's a wilderness; to me, it's paradise.

I make the pilgrimage several times each spring, starting early so that I can reach the moorland before dawn. Then, I sit quietly in the heather, watching and waiting. Almost at once, I hear the horse-neighing sound of snipe displaying above my head, and as the first light hits the horizon, blackcocks assemble to dance like crazy turkeys. On a fine morning, there's no better sight than watching these unique birds displaying in a group to attract a mate. It's just like a disco. However, in the world of birds, it's the males that do the dancing whilst the females choose the mate!

No spring morning is quite perfect without hearing the call of the curlew, although this species is getting scarcer all over Wales these days. If I'm lucky, I can watch a large whitish-grey bird with black wing-tips flying low over the heather in search of prey. This is a male hen harrier, the most beautiful bird of prey in Europe, and even though it's a rare bird, it can be seen occasionally on the Migneint. Here and there, red grouse call and Llyn Conwy's gulls fly back and forth from the fields below where they feed on worms and all sorts of insects.

Hot days are good for moths, especially the silver or bronze-coloured Emperor with those large eyes on its wings. Amidst the white moss is the sundew, a plant that has adapted to catch insects because there are very few nutrients in the peat, and by the end of spring, bog cotton waves its white heads in the wind. Farmland birds of prey, like the kestrel and the buzzard, come to hunt the mountain and today, Wales's national bird, the red kite, has re-established itself in the natural community.

Yes, all this wildlife is there to be seen and heard on the heather-covered hills of the Migneint. But even a wet and windy day, when any sensible bird is lying low, is a boon for me, as long as I can escape to the wilderness of this remote mountain, away from work, away from people and away from the world and its problems.

Iolo Williams

Craig Goch and the Migneint.

AFON DWYRYD

I am cheating by describing a journey rather than a place: a journey by canoe down the Dwyryd river, starting where it meets the A487 just below Plas Tan-y-Bwlch. A relatively high tide is needed to canoe, the best time to start being just before the tide turns – the dwell time. Some knowledge of canoeing, tides, currents and so on are essential for this journey. However, also essential for me are a flask of coffee and a box of cakes!

As I set off downriver, steeply-wooded slopes reach up each side of me, on the left to the Rhinogydd and, on the right, the summit of Moelwyn Bach is just visible. Winding my way downstream with the dark shapes of Manod Bach and Manod Mawr behind me, I come to the old wharf at Gelli Grin where the barges used to collect the slate from the quarries of Blaenau Ffestiniog and deliver them to the sailing ships in Porthmadog harbour. Now crumbling and deserted, it is hard to imagine how busy it once used to be.

Ahead, the wooded slopes open out slightly to give a sense of more space, whilst Brewett bridge, carrying the railway over the estuary, dominates the view. Because of the relatively small bridge with broad, close-together wooden legs, the water rushes through the narrow gap. Passing under it is always exciting, sometimes even quite scary.

Shooting out from under the bridge, the landscape changes dramatically into the wide open expanse of the estuary. On the left, Harlech castle can be seen in silhouette and on the right is Traeth Penrhyn, where, as children, we used to build dams at the mouth of one of the many streams in a vain attempt to stop the tide. (Needless to say, all we succeeded in doing was angering the local farmer). Above, Cnicht and the Moelwynion now stand bathed in sunlight.

The river swings left and ahead of me lies the lovely little island, Ynys Gifftan, always a good place to land and have coffee and cake. You can find shelter from the wind whatever its direction, with an equally good view wherever you choose to sit. From here I head out towards Portmeirion's lighthouse, passing the village on my right as I embark on the final leg of my journey.

Rounding the point of the lighthouse, the land on my left drops away to leave nothing but long sandbanks between the open sea and me. On my right the tropical-looking wooded slopes of Trwyn Penrhyn slowly recede to reveal the stunning view into the Snowdonia National Park where Moel Ddu, Moel Hebog, Yr Wyddfa, Cnicht and the Moelwynion are looking their very best.

Now there is just the paddle into the harbour at Porthmadog, back to this hectic life that we all lead. But at least I have the peace that my journey has given me to carry me through until the next one.

SIAN ROBERTS

Afon Dwyryd and the Moelwynion.

LLYN TEGID

When T.H. Parry-Williams said that bits of him lay scattered over the place, he was referring to one place – the place of his early years in Rhyd-ddu. I feel something similar myself, except in my case, the bits are scattered in many places: Brynaman at the foot of the Black Mountain, Aberhosan near Machynlleth, Cwm Tydu and Llangrannog, and the land between Snowdonia and the sea where I have spent most of the past thirty years.

But there is one other place from which I cannot escape, and that is Penllyn where I spent my teenage years. My home was in Llanuwchllyn, and the school was in Bala, and between them is Wales's largest natural lake, Llyn Tegid. Every morning, it was my privilege to walk to Llanuwchllyn's little station to catch the one-carriage train to school.

That must have been one of the world's best school runs! The little train (it's now officially a 'little train' but in those days it was just a small train on a big line) travelled along the fringe of the lake almost the whole way from Llanuwchllyn, through Llangywer, to Bala Junction. Every day, the nature of the lake was different. On some days, the wind whipped the surface into angry waves. At other times, it was deep blue, reflecting the summer sky. On some days the lake was like a mirror, reflecting every tree and hill clearly, its surface broken only by the perfect lines of a wild duck's wake.

Adding to the magic were the area's rich associations. Not far from the station stood Coed-y-pry, boyhood home of Sir O.M. Edwards, and across the lake stood Glan-llyn, the Urdd Centre. The whole area had been introduced to me through the evocative words of Llew Tegid in the folk song *'Ffarwel i Blwy Llangywer'* ('Farewell to the Parish of Llangywer'). How could an innocent youngster not lose his heart to such a place!

But it was not all legend and song. In Llangywer Vicarage lived and worked a real live poet, the enigmatic Euros Bowen. Every morning the little train waited patiently for the door of the Vicarage to open and the poet's son, Huw, to emerge late for school. Further along, through the windows of that single carriage, during the 1950s I saw, between the Junction and Bala itself, work being done on the course of the Tryweryn River to prepare the way for the momentous damming of the Valley. Wales was never the same after that.

DAFYDD IWAN

Llanuwchllyn station.

Four Ruins and a Reservoir in a Place across the Mountain

My favourite short walk in Snowdonia, which always reminds me of our historic impact on the landscape, begins and ends at one of those small but perfectly formed SNP car parks near Tomen-y-Mur. It's only a mile round this thirty-acre site of Roman military remains from the first century – a fort with later boundary walls, an amphitheatre, a Roman officer's bath-house and burial mounds. A later addition is the medieval motte or castle, the *tomen* of the site name. Later again is a farmhouse built from Roman dressed stone, an early use of secondary aggregate! Then there are the industrial buildings of the seventeenth century, the leat to the Tyddyn Du cornmill, and the nineteenth-century tramway route to Braich Ddu quarry. Here, as all over Snowdonia, are remains which speak to us of our heritage in slate quarrying and mineral extraction. It was those same minerals which probably brought the Romans and their legions here in the first place to these highlands they named Eryri. Meanwhile, the inhabitants of what was to become Trawsfynydd, the place across the mountain, carried on speaking, then writing a British language which became Welsh!

The small Roman amphitheatre is interesting but the greatest amphitheatre is formed by the mountain ranges themselves – Cader Idris to the south, Rhinogydd to the west, Moelwynion and Manod, with their great mounds of slate to the north with Allt Fawr beyond. Back towards the south-east, forestry plantations cover the former military ranges of the twentieth-century British Army.

But the centrepiece of our stage is the great reservoir of Trawsfynydd. By it sits Snowdonia's finest and biggest 'ruin' of all, the buildings of Trawsfynydd Nuclear Power Station, naked to our eyes now that the great turbine hall with its monster machinery has been taken away.

Llyn Trawsfynydd's main dam was built in the 1920s to provide water for an earlier hydro scheme at Maentwrog. Twenty-four cottages and the ubiquitous chapel were demolished and the great bog, y Gors Goch, with its magic flora and fauna, was drained. An enormous catchment area was created with leats and ditches as well as Afon Prysor itself. Then in the 1960s, very much in my time, the lake was drained again to build Britain's only inland magnox station. This is when the archipelago of islands was constructed to facilitate the circulation of warmed waters.

As we walk this short round, we cannot fail to be reminded how human impact on this planet and its ecology is all a series of *tomenni* ('mounds') constructed by human labour from generation to generation. No landscape can ever escape this. All landscape is created, even if it wasn't part of Creation, here in Eryri above all.

Dafydd Elis Thomas

Industrial relics, Trawsfynydd.

CWM BEUDY MAWR

This is a special place. A wilderness so close to humanity; a path above, a road below, a bustling car-park a few hundred yards away. But you will not meet the casual walker here. It is a place to sit and stare.

Beneath my boots, the green and brown divide into a multitude of grasses, mosses and bilberry. Through the green, speckles of colour appear: bright yellow tormentil, soft blue milkwort and exotic red sundew. The longer you look, the more colour and flowers appear.

Around me the land is complicated, with bumps and hollows adorned with crags and water. This is a busy place on the map, full of lines and shapes fascinating to the map-reader. It is a place for trainers and assessors of navigation.

Beyond, the valley drops and climbs to the sunshine. The slopes here are rough, textured by heather and rock. For most of the year green and grey but, for a few months, they smoulder purple with heather.

From these slopes dark cliffs protrude. These are my favourite places. They are not still but full of movement, life and personal drama. From here, climbers are a cluster of coloured dots at the cliff base or an individual dash of colour slowly moving its way up a vertical and apparently blank wall. Each one is involved in its own physical puzzle surrounded by space and lost in time. Suddenly there is a change of pace. Someone reaches the top and waves frantically to the sky. I am too far to hear the call but close enough to know the emotion.

Above me other slopes rise steeply to ridges and summits. This is where to find company and a different view. I have a view but only the wind as companion.

Time passes. The sunlight drifts away down the Pass turning the valley grey. The light and colour are now my horizon, beyond is the sea and sky.

It is a place I have visited often. I have come here to work and come for leisure.

It is a place just to be.

LOUISE THOMAS

Stormy day, Nant Peris.

Y BRYNIAU MELYNION

Codwn ac awn i geisio'r Bryniau Melynion,
A'u cyrchu drwy'r fawnog hyd lwybr cynefin i'n traed.
Dyrchafwn ein llygaid rhag dinistr balchder dynion,
Rhag tân olynydd metalaidd y bicell waed.
Syllwn ar lun y copaon yn y merddwr llonydd
Wrth fwrw trem ein myfyr dros gerddediad ein byw brith.
Mor fach y teimlwn yng nghysgod hynafol y bronnydd,
Yn ehangder y gweundir drwy'r tes yn crynu fel rhith.
Oedwn i wylio'r brithyll yn llithro dan dorlannau,
A'r pelydrau'n pefrio dawns ar y crawcwellt sych,
Cyn dringo'n sicr i greigiau clir yr uchelfannau
Yn dyrau dyrchafol uwchlaw'r dyfroedd di-grych.
Cyrraedd, a theimlo'r awelon sy'n cylchu'r cread,
Aros i'w hanadl buro a bywhau ein gwead.

Bryniau Melynion are the hills opposite Ysgolion Duon at the far end of Cwm Pen Llafar between Carnedd Llywelyn and Carnedd Dafydd. A path follows the Llafar river and the stream of Nant y Gilfach Felen past Bryniau Melynion and through the pass of Bwlch y Clawdd Llwyd to the summit of Carnedd Llywelyn.

When we were children, the remains of a war plane were scattered over this slope, with parts on the banks and in the pools of Nant y Gilfach Felen. We used to carry and drag them down the mountainside.

The poem encourages us to raise our sights above the mire of familiar routine, and to seek that which elevates us. The war plane symbolizes our failure to resolve disputes without resorting to war, and is a successor to the blood-stained pike and the primitive spear.

To avoid violence and war, we need to follow the path that leads us to the spirit which elevates the soul, the path that takes us from the flat ordinariness of life to summits of spiritual meaning and values. The winds that have always circled the planet symbolize the spirit.

IEUAN WYN

Yr Elen and Afon Llafar.

THE SNOWDON LILY IN ERYRI

It is like meeting old friends. I have more than once caught myself smiling broadly, saying hello and almost expecting a handshake. This is no accidental meeting, however. There is the long walk uphill with a heavy sack, the scramble to set up ropes, putting on enough clothes to keep warm for the three hours or more I shall spend roped to the cold north-facing cliff and finally ensuring I have all the survey equipment tied to me, so it can't fall to the bottom of the cliff whilst I'm still near the top. All this occupies my mind fully, so that it is only when I am tied onto the rope and sliding down slowly to the first site that I remember why I am really here and why I go through this ritual each year to greet my old friends. I do it as a scientist to monitor plants, but there is something more.

Old friend is a somewhat misleading description for this delicate wisp of a plant which has survived on its cliff sites in Eryri, though nowhere else in Britain, for the past 10,000 years. You would imagine a puff of wind would break the slender stem and leaves, yet it occupies some of the steepest and coldest terrain in the Eryri mountains, growing in the smallest crevices and living on the remnants of its old leaves and whatever nutrients it can extract from the rocks and the rain.

Surveying its cousins in America and the European Mountains is a different experience. Here it grows in abundance on gently rolling alpine tundra amidst an excess of other colourful plant species. Hot sun during the summer and snow-cover or harsh desiccating winds in the winter are the character-forming elements it must deal with in this environment.

It is a survivor, possibly even remaining in Wales on isolated 'islands' of rock during the last ice advances. This ability to survive may become crucial for *Lloydia* in Wales in the next 100 or so years. We have collected it for our herbaria in the past, confined it through heavy grazing pressures in the present and, through climate change, we may be altering its environment for the future. Will it continue to grace our cliffs in Eryri? I hope so, but it will need help from us. Help to enable it to spread outwards from its current confines, to increase in numbers and improve its chances of surviving whatever new challenges we may throw at it in the future. Never take old friends for granted.

BARBARA JONES

The Snowdon Lily (*Lloydia serotina*).

THE GLYDERAU

I first saw the Glyderau in 1947. My mother and father, Chris and Jo Briggs, and I were on our way from Manchester to start a new life at the Pen-y-Gwryd hotel, nestling under Glyder Fach. I was four years old and had never seen a mountain before. It was a glorious day and, as we rounded the corner in Capel Curig, the sight took my breath away. It started a love affair that continues to this day.

My father was very involved in mountain rescue in the early days. He would come into the hotel and ask for volunteers, even if we were sitting down to dinner, to go with him! It was a great honour that when he died, a helicopter from RAF Valley took us up onto the Glyderau to scatter his ashes within sight of Pen-y-Gwryd.

Our next-door neighbours, Esme and Peter Kirby, used to farm at Dyffryn Mymbyr and owned the Glyderau. Since they died, the farm has been gifted to the National Trust. We often used to help them gather the sheep. Esme was the heroine of *I Bought a Mountain* – a book about our valley which has been translated into many different languages.

In the 57 years I have lived at the Pen-y-Gwryd, I have come to know the mountain in all its different moods – in spring, covered in new lambs; in summer, purple with heather; and in winter, white and inaccessible with ice and snow. There are the most wonderful rock formations on the plateau at the top, quite unlike anything found on the other mountains. Some look like castles – hence Castell-y-Gwynt – and one is a huge cantilever much photographed with people sitting on its far end.

There is a lake, Llyn Cwmffynnon, in the bowl of the mountain. As the stream, Nant Gwryd, wanders down the valley from the lake, it forms a crystal-clear rock-pool, in which we have bathed for many years. It's like bathing in silk. Our water supply also comes direct from the Glyderau. It's so wonderfully soft that people have been known to bring their cashmere sweaters from London to wash them in PYG water!

When I lie in my bed, I am able to look out of the window and see the Glyderau and their different and changing moods. Today they are covered with snow and looking as magnificent as any Alpine or Himalayan peak. I shall never tire of them.

JANE PULLEE

Afon Gwryd and the Glyderau.

THE MOELWYNION AND RHOSYDD

When I was a child, my favourite teacher was a naturalist. One day he showed us his slides of a magical bird that nested inside old quarry tunnels. It had a flame-red, slightly curved bill, red legs and bright, bright eyes. High above Moel yr Hydd, it would tumble, drop and dive, playing in the wind, its calls echoing plaintively. Sitting cross-legged, absorbed in the life of this bird, I became aware for the first time of another world around me. I wanted to go where this magical bird flew in freedom above the tawny slopes of mountains I looked up to every day.

A few years later, I stood in the middle of Bwlch Rhosydd. Alone, I turned a slow circle. First I saw the steep slopes of Allt y Ceffylau plunging into the unseen mysterious waters of Llyn Cwmorthin. Northwards, an undulating land redolent with poetry – Conglog, Corsiog, Clogwyn Brith, Boethwel and Dafydd y Foel. Turning slowly, I looked at Cnicht. I felt I could almost touch it. Beyond lay Cwm Croesor with its promise of oak woods and hidden valleys. My eyes swept down the slopes of Cnicht and up to the gentle dome of Moelwyn Mawr. To me these summits were unassailable, remote. Sacred, even. Turning again, my eyes rested on the ruins of quarrymen's homes, the windows and doorways still resonant with memories, before returning to Cwmorthin. It was very quiet up there. The quality of the silence was unique, a church for the past, a haven for the present.

I sat on the warm slate and looked at the map. Why this yellow line? It came southwards from Corsiog, marched through Bwlch Rhosydd, embraced Moel yr Hydd, made a dip as it headed east towards Manod, northwards to the Penmachno quarries and finally back west over the Crimea to Druman. It's a circle, signifying exclusion and rejection of land not worthy of respect or National Park status. I looked down into Cwm Orthin again and I turned to gaze on Cnicht. I puzzled at this statement of partition and difference, feeling only a sense of unity, of belonging, in a land whose wildness was on a grand enough scale to absorb the weathered scars of its quarried past.

Many years later I stood again on the same spot. It had become a battleground splitting a community in two. The yellow line had allowed battle lines to be drawn: on the one side those who wanted to re-open Cwm Orthin and Rhosydd as a working quarry, right up towards the Moelwyn summit; on the other side, those who felt this to be a fundamental betrayal of an ideal and a landscape.

Our community is still absorbing the scars. The yellow line is still on the map. The choughs, those magical birds, still wheel high above the Moelwynion.

RONWEN ROBERTS

On the yellow line, the Moelwynion.

LLYN ELSI

On many evenings and Sunday afternoons, my family and I with our two labradors, Celyn and Bear, walk up from our home to the monument at Llyn Elsi above Betws-y-coed. It's our backyard.

My children love the walk. Cai, now six, runs ahead as he knows all the paths, calling to me when he's found something interesting – a frog, a new badger-trail, wild strawberries. Finn, his younger brother usually trails behind, playing in puddles or throwing sticks for the dogs. At the monument we stop for chocolate.

From here you can see over most of the Gwydyr Forest – from Crafnant in the north, round to Bryn Engan on the flanks of Moel Siabod, and the slopes of Drosgl and Ro-wen above Penmachno in the south. The kids climb to the top of the monument. Excitedly, they tell us they can see the first mountain they climbed, Crimpiau, at the end of Llyn Crafnant, and they list the bigger mountains they're going to climb one day.

I look at 'my' forest and think how lucky I am to live and work here. My only regret is that my father never saw our home, as it was he who took me as a young boy for evening walks through a forest, and gave me the love of trees that led to my becoming a forester.

KIM BURNHAM

Autumn light in the Gwydyr, Moel Siabod beyond.

HIDDEN BY THE HILLSIDE

In the dark I can hear sheep moving all around me. Occasionally one will call to its lambs then, apart from the wind, all will be quiet for a while.

In front of me, I can make out the shape of the north end of the Rhinogydd – Moel Penolau, Moel Ysgyfarnogod and Bryn Cader Faner.

To the east is the unmistakable outline of the Moelwynion and Cnicht. High on the hillsides are the lights of houses and farms scattered around Croesor village. Between Moelwyn Bach and Moelwyn Mawr is the orange glow of the streetlights of Blaenau Ffestiniog, nine miles away on a straight line.

To the north is Snowdon where, on clear summer nights, the light from the summit station can be seen.

To the west, beyond the curve of the old sea cliffs at Tremadog, lie Porthmadog and the open sea. On nights before bad weather, I can sit here and sounds from miles away carry clearly on the air. An occasional car will pass on the road, the headlights giving warning as they are reflected on the wooded hillsides. Behind me, the slope is thickly wooded with a mixture of sessile oak and ash, which makes an unbroken belt from the National Nature Reserve at Tremadog to the Aberglaslyn Pass.

Hidden by the hillside is our farm. Surrounded by old stone buildings, it shelters the fourth generation of our family to farm this land.

KATHRYN DAVIES

Fron Oleu, the Moelwynion beyond.

THE DYSYNNI VALLEY

We all live in a landscape, though its quality may vary considerably; but so will our personal interpretation of what surrounds us – the landscape of our minds.

My favourite location is where I live, at the bottom of the Dysynni Valley, one of the gateways to the National Park. From our land near the river, on the wide valley floor, a distant Cader Idris faces me. To my right the valley splits; the runs of rounded hills becoming bleaker as they roll inland to form the Tal-y-llyn Pass. On either side, fields and *ffridd* carved by generations of farmers; whilst behind my back lie the flat marsh lands, sea and sky.

It is a stunning place. But its impact is deeper than visual gratification: this place touches the landscape of my mind.

Part is touched by its openness. Half this landscape is empty, an untouched canvas of blue sky and sea, waiting for new ideas like unformed cloud formations to come rolling by. And in the distance, holy Bardsey balances on the horizon, oscillating between my eyes and imagination.

Part is touched by change. This is not a static landscape. Over time, sea and tide, silt and sand have changed a vast estuary to a fertile valley, a natural process aided by sweat, cunning and ingenuity to form productive and scenic farmland whose stone walls, hedges, fields and mountain enclosures trace the undulating fortunes of hundreds of years of agriculture. Only the cormorants remain untouched, flying daily from Craig yr Aderyn to fish the sea, oblivious to the fact that their inland home has long since ceased to be a tide-swept rock. And further up, Castell y Bere stands at the valley's end, its strategic position now landlocked and in ruins.

Part is touched by unimaginable force. My stunning landscape was caused by a major geological fault, the Bala cleft, that created Tal-y-llyn lake and Llyn Tegid and by volcanic activity whose remnants formed Cader Idris and the out-of-sight Rhobell Fawr. This was followed in geological time by recent glaciation that split, smoothed and eroded the passive hills around me.

This is my favourite location, so soothing and appealing but created by force and destruction; maintained by renewal and decay; brought alive in the landscape of my mind. And, for an iota of time in its evolution, my home.

ANNE LLOYD-JONES

Fault line, the Dysynni valley.

FROM THE TOP OF CNICHT

The sea is visible from the top of Cnicht – not that I am a sea-lover at all, far from it. I just want to make sure it is still out there and that the coast from Dyffryn Ardudwy to Penrhyn Llŷn, my beautiful home bay, continues, like a rampart, to keep it out. The sea has its place, though, as a door from my world to the rest of the world, which is essential to my well-being.

Between the sea and Cnicht lies Traeth Mawr, the wetland retrieved from the sea by William Alexander Maddocks in 1812. Looking inland from the Cob, Maddocks's rampart, Cnicht indubitably stands out. Guidebooks say that the name is derived from the word 'knight' because the mountain resembles a knight's helmet but, surely, that stems from Victorian bowdlerisation. I regard it as a Celtic phenomenon, thrusting into the sky from the tangle of clefts, trees and bushes at its root.

Evidence abounds of its violent origins. Nearby, glowering quietly, is Yr Arddu, composed of shards of volcanic rocks erupted from the bowels of the earth. Between eruptions, mud was forming beneath the sea from which emerged the characteristic stone of the area – the slate, the 'blue vein' that flowed from the clay of the sea as that was squeezed, burnt and cooked once, twice and thrice over. From the area of Cnicht – from Croesor, Rhosydd, Cwm Orthin – the blue, waterproof cover that would roof houses worldwide was transported by sea from Porthmadog, the door opened by Maddocks.

Then there are the *cymoedd* – each cwm, originally formed by ice, opened doors to the sea – and Cwm Croesor is a classic. More recently in the history of the world, they have defined routes for mankind: a track, a tramway, an incline, a road and a path in the National Park.

There is so much activity to be seen with the mind's eye from the top of Cnicht. And yet it is so tranquil. In that great stillness the lakes glitter and two black-backed gulls sweep gracefully on the mountain breeze, their backs shining in the sun. They are silent, so different from their ruckus when flocking together. Not unlike people, in fact. Thank goodness then for the croak of the raven, a real inhabitant of the mountain.

And it is a crowd of mountains that keep me company – Snowdon and its satellites, Glyderau, Carneddau, Moel Siabod, Hebog, Arennig Fawr and Arennig Fach; and in the distance, the ridge of Cader Idris, southern sentinel of Snowdonia. This silent crowd reverberates with the history of my land, its despair and its hopes.

Mountain and sea, plains and ridges, creation and destruction, ramparts and gateways – they are all a magnificent muddle in the head and heart of the little Welshman on the top of Cnicht.

MERFYN WILLIAMS

Cwm Croesor and the coast from Cnicht.

DYFFRYN NANT FFRANCON

I've been tenant for eight years now at Blaen-y-Nant, an uplands organic farm in Dyffryn Nant Ffrancon. This is a paradise created by God (with a little help from humans) – craggy mountains, fantastic open wilderness, stone-walled fields, screes, a lovely winding river. To me it's the most special place on earth.

Being here reminds me of when I was a little boy. We children used to congregate during the summer holidays to play outside in the woods, the stream or the meadows – no foreign holidays then, no computer, no TV. I remember the smell of haymaking, gone now because hay has been replaced by silage and even the meadow grasses have changed.

When I was growing up, the area was very quiet. As we were gathering the sheep, we only ever saw a few hardened walkers in their hobnailed boots. All we heard were the voices of other shepherds, commanding their dogs or talking to one another. Nowadays I might see 200-300 walkers in a day, and if I whistle my dog, I might have fifty children whistling with me! Which is great, actually, because I'm trying to bring them into the farm.

I think it's important to bring country and city folk together. Visitors these days don't have contact with locals like they used to. My grandparents' way of diversifying their farm's income was to have B&B. At that time people came for the whole week, by train to Bangor. They brought bikes with them and spent their time in

the area, cycling and enjoying the scenery. By the end of the week they were more like relatives and friends. I'm trying to recreate that kind of experience, and also to encourage schools to visit the nature walk we've built at the bottom of the valley.

I love improving the farm so that it's a better environment for wildlife. I get immense pleasure from seeing work done that's been neglected for a hundred years or so, recreating old field boundaries, re-establishing woodlands and seeing wildlife return to them.

I could never live in a city and work in a factory. This is my life, living in the mountains and shepherding. But I want to *share* the farm with the factory worker from the city – so I want it to be at its best all the time.

Gwyn Thomas

Summer evening, Nant Ffrancon.

To Llyn Anafon

Leaving my home I drop down into the Nant, which has been Llanfairfechan's main artery for over a thousand years. Ascending on the other side, I am soon skirting the National Park boundary and, if moving west, approaching Bryn Goleu. This farmhouse, like so many, is an extraordinary collection of buildings of various dates. I turn left and make a sharp climb up the old track around the shoulder of Garreg Fawr, which was part of the important Stone-axe complex and which has one of the multi-cellular sheepfolds unique to the Carneddau.

The track soon meets the Roman Road and I can look back at Bwlch y Ddeufaen or towards Aber. Although I had walked the road many times and had its origins thoroughly explained to me, I never really understood it until I became a soldier. Often, on the breeze, I can hear a cohort coming over the rise out of Nant Conwy and, seeing Penmaenmawr for the first time, hear the old sweats terrifying the younger recruits with tales of 'what that lot over there will do to you if they get their hands on you!'. Walking under the 400-kilovolt pylons, I think of that First-world-war veteran – and my eight-year-old legs hurrying alongside his as we climbed to gather mountain ponies.

I continue on the track towards Drum with a head almost overflowing with memories. The years have erased the number of times I have made this journey but they have not changed the joy of it. I drove up this track almost every day for three months in 1964 whilst building the Foel Grach Refuge. But the pleasure of seeing the ponies, or one of the mountain men, clothes held together with baling twine, surrounded by darting dogs, has never diminished.

The track climbs round Foel Ganol and soon Carnedd Pen-y-dorth Goch comes into view. A quick walk over the dwarf shrub heath, often disturbing a group of ponies, and you are looking down into Llyn Anafon. Rarely does it appear sunny, even on the best of days, and the rocks above on Llwytmor are often menacing. The Carneddau can be a very wild and lonely place. Two members of the local Home Guard died from exposure whilst on exercise here and, about the same time, two young children went missing nearer Penmaenmawr. Bloodhounds were brought in from Scotland Yard to help in the search. How things have changed! Penmaenmawr now has its own search dogs.

It is strange that these mountains, encapsulating much of the history of the earth and seeming so unchanging, have witnessed so much change about them. In days gone by, I often passed this spot on my way to the higher mountains of the Carneddau. These days, I am more likely to stay at the shoulder and gaze at the Llyn and the rocks and maybe ponder a little, hoping also to see the ponies and one of the locals whom I will surely know.

WARREN MARTIN

Llyn Anafon and Llwytmor from Pen Bryn-du.

TOUCHSTONE – AFON CYNFAL, VALE OF FFESTINIOG

Up on the Migneint, the waters of Afon Goch, Nant y Groes and Afon Las converge near Pont yr Afon Gam to become the Cynfal, flowing west towards the Vale of Ffestiniog. Water stained by peat to a rich ale tan foams through rapids and plunges down Rhaeadr-y-Cwm to a steep-sided, wooded valley, through dark gullies and rocks dense with moss.

In a quiet stretch, after the last major falls and before meeting the Dwyryd, sits a massive rock, ten tons of granite, six feet high. Seen from downstream, it has a square block form, from upstream it is domed; perched in a way that makes it appear awake and aware of its singularity – a brooding authority. Covered in thick moss, with a dark underside, it overhangs the rapid flow of the Cynfal.

I first met this rock aged six or seven, the youngest by far of a group of boys venturing as high as we could along the Cynfal from the bottom of Allt Goch below Llan Ffestiniog. A difficult scramble, stumbling over wet and slippery rocks. Suddenly we were in the presence of this 'rock-being'. It was my first sculpture-experience – that is, experiencing an inanimate object speaking its presence. There are other single rocks, obstacles to go round or over, but this rock is unique. For fifty years I have visited it and, trying to articulate my art, taken museum curators and art writers to see it. For me it is perfect in its simplicity, a primal object that by nature, time, size, environment and placement is a 'touchstone' for my path as a sculptor.

DAVID NASH

CWM PENNANT

There is a famous, and rather sentimental, poem by Eifion Wyn, which poses this question:

Pam, Arglwydd, y gwnaethost Gwm Pennant mor dlws
A bywyd hen fugail mor fyr?

('Why, Lord, did you make Cwm Pennant so lovely/
And an old shepherd's life so short?')

The thought is commonplace enough, though no less affecting for that. But the location is sublime. Through the years I lived here, the sense grew on me of a landscape thick with ghosts, where generations had arranged and re-arranged stones into the temporary shapes of two or three hundred years, borrowed from here to build there, let frost and wind collapse and the grass wipe clean: '*Mae lleisiau a drychiolaethau ar hyd y lle*', wrote Parry-Williams – voices and phantoms throughout the place. It is one of the loveliest valleys in this most lovely of all countries: streams and woods, close turf with orchids and scabious, church and chapel, ridge and dome of hill, a drift of bluebells like woodsmoke across a green shade.

For me the people were as much a part of it as river or hills. These were the old faces, the lingering conversations, all the companionable crises of the farmer's year: the frenetic sweat and itch of stacking hay, pandemonious sadism at dipping, the shepherding – a time in the late snow, the ewe tired with long labour, no option but to bare my arm to the elbow, push the breech lamb up and round before pulling it out, lamb and my arm both marbled bloody and yellow against the white ground. A few days later, in a field now patched with green, I saw a hare rear up to box with this same lamb.

I remember talking with old Mr Morus, Gilfach, asking why sheep's heads hung in the trees above the stream by his house: '*Duw*, it's cure for the *pendro*. When the sheeps die, I cut off its head and hang it there. Blowfly lays eggs, maggots eat the brain, fall into the stream, and the sickness is washed from the land.'

You'll not find beliefs like that current in Cwm Pennant these days. Acre-millionaires, seekers of subsidies, have bought into the valley. The land wire-fenced, huge grey wintering sheds dominate. It is made to work, to repay investment in it. Rather than this exploitation, I am not sure that I do not prefer a certain old Calvinist unease at its beauty, which spoke at least of the power and mystery of place, and a certain reverence.

JIM PERRIN

Spring in Cwm Pennant.

MOEL SIABOD

To start life in its shadow and, over three-quarters of a century later, still to be living and admiring the view of my favourite mountain, Moel Siabod, is fortune experienced by a rare few. I was born, the seventh child of the quarry manager, at its foot in Pont Cyfyng, a small community of quarry workers and their families. How things have changed! Everyone there in my young days spoke Welsh, and everyone, bar one family, was a chapel-goer. The quarry, now closed and on private land, was a wonderful place to grow up and to learn about people and life. Situated on the lower slopes of the mountain, we had a unique introduction to Moel Siabod and the lower valley of the river Llugwy.

Water running off Moel Siabod was collected and turned the water wheel which supplied the power for the quarry shed. It then ran on to the Llugwy where my brothers and I fished for trout. All my three brothers were fishermen, but I learnt the art from my nearest brother, John, sadly killed in the war. Our favourite stretch was from Pont Cyfyng down to the stepping stones and beyond to the little stream that runs down from Bryn Gefeiliau. The ever-changing view towards Moel Siabod never failed to inspire and reassure us.

We fished in all weathers. A flood with brown water meant a day worm-fishing the big pool below the falls at Pont Cyfyng. With plenty of fish to be caught, there was no need to move on. At other times, before the leaves came on the trees, we fished the moving water with a fly. The hungry trout, hunting for food, took the fly greedily. Our first trip down the river at the start of the season, towards the stepping stones, meant carrying a saw to cut gaps in the growing trees so that we could cast the fly. The next flood took away the cut-down branches. Once the leaves were out, we fished the mountain lakes, Llyn y Foel on Siabod and Llyn Newydd, the quarry lake, being favourites.

For a brief period in June or July it was possible to find live *coch y bonddu* beetles on the bracken in some areas. These were incredibly good for catching trout. They were put on a hook and, with a short line and much crawling, 'dapped' on to the surface of the water near the bank and under the trees. Sometimes the trout, sheltering under the bank or in the shadows, would leap at the bait before it reached the water. It was all very exciting and for some reason seemed to entice bigger fish. All this pleasure, available to a youngster then, is denied everyone today, including me, because of the lack of fish. Acid rain has killed off the insects that they used to feed on. Even the mountain lakes have suffered.

But I still live in Capel Curig and still look out at my favourite mountain. I am so lucky.

OWEN WYN OWEN

Flowing shapes and stepping stones, Afon Llugwy.

GLOYWLYN

My choice had to be in Meirionnydd, for no other area in the whole of Wales can offer such a wide variety of beautiful natural features.

But where in Meirionnydd? There were certain conditions I wanted to meet. The choice had to be a completely natural feature, untouched by man, and set in an area where there was little, if any, evidence that things had changed since the ice moved away. So, no buildings, no roads, no planted forest, and no fertilised fields. Tough conditions these days, but in the wonderfully beautiful area west of the Rhinog range of mountains, they can be met. From this range, four rivers flow west to the sea and all have stunningly attractive features in their journeys. My selection is a lake high up on the south side of one of the river valleys, Afon Artro.

No road reaches the lake, of course, and some careful map-reading is needed to find it. It is positioned in an isolated cradle of rock set below the impressive bulk of Rhinog Fawr. There are a number of ways of reaching it. It is possible to descend from Rhinog Fawr, past Llyn Du, and then continue down with the fine view of the lake below. If a rocky scramble is favoured, then one can go up Carreg-y-Saeth and savour the view of the lake from high above yet very close to it. There are other routes, but my favourite keeps the jewel hidden right till the last moment.

It starts alongside the Artro near Cwm-yr-Afon farm, takes the old mineral track which climbs up the gentle slope of the valley side and gives wonderful views. The track is left when it reaches a small plateau, and the route continues up along one side of a broad, shallow, subsidiary valley containing an outlet stream from my mountain lake, which makes its way down to join the Artro. The scenery is wild and dramatic: boulders and steep-faced outcrops, much heather and a mixture of other moorland plants, but no hint of the lake hidden higher above. The climb continues up as far as a final rim of rock. There, suddenly, breathtakingly, Gloywlyn is revealed. William Condry wrote 'Long may it remain, unexploited, tranquil and remote, for the spirit of man needs such retreats.' Mine certainly does.

GEOFF ELLIOTT

Clearing storm, Gloywlyn.

From Penmaen Rock

My favourite view in the Snowdonia National Park is that from the top of Penmaen rock – between Bronaber and Ganllwyd, looking down at my home, Ffridd Bryn Coch Farm, with the Rhinogydd in the background.

When I was a child, Taid and Dad were the ones running the farm, and at every opportunity I would be at their shirt-tails feeding the sheep, or collecting hay bales on the back of the little red Nuffield. I still have many sweet memories of my *taid* such as the old weather signs he used. Even now, when it is time to bring the sheep from the mountain, Dad looks up to the tops of the Rhinogydd searching for a cloud-cap that would indicate rain. Or he'll look over to the Crawcwellt river for the wild horses. If they're really close to the river, this too will be a sign of rain.

It was at home on the farm that my interest in wildlife started. I was coming home from school one day and met the late Ted Breeze Jones and his wife, Anwen. Ted had found, in one of the old cowsheds, a barn owl's nest containing some chicks which, at the time, seemed quite ugly. There are still owls in the cowshed, and I continue to care for them. Like many others, I too caught Ted's enthusiasm.

Today, my brother and father work the farm. Farming has been modernising for a while, but over the last ten years, the farm has altered also in favour of wildlife through a number of conservation projects. There are more birds to see, for example, skylarks, grey wagtails, stonechats, dippers, hen harriers, merlins, grouse and, recently, a nightjar. And one of my favourite mammals on the river is, of course, the otter.

This will be my back garden for an age: the pastures and the Rhinogydd. As Iwan Morgan says:

> *Hen Ddrws caregog is y Rhinogau,*
> *Ei annedd anial a'm swynodd innau;*
> *Y mae i ŵr hyd ei noethlwm erwau*
> *Le i hir gilio'n ei gêl rigolau;*
> *Hen hanes sy'n ei haenau, – fe'i gwelir*
> *Yn hud a miri'r rhyfedd dymhorau.*

Sarah Jones

Sunrise, Ffridd Bryn Coch farm.

Llyn Tegid and Bala

Llyn Tegid is the largest natural lake in Wales – and I love it! Coming from Lesotho, a dry mountainous country where you don't see much water, I'm delighted to live and work so close to the lake. I can see it from my living room. I see it every morning when I get up and before I go to bed.

The views change with the seasons. It's lovely, especially in the summer with a blue sky above the water. And yet, it scares me sometimes in the winter when we get a lot of flooding in Bala. It hasn't affected us yet but last winter it came uncomfortably close to our house. However, we walk along the lake every evening: myself, my husband, my six-year-old son – and our sheepdog, who absolutely loves water. No matter what time of the year it is, he will go for a swim!

In the summer we picnic by the lake sometimes. At that time of year it's really busy. Although you might expect just tourists then, we also see lots of locals who sit down for a chat. There are quite a few activities on the lake, what with canoeing, sailing and swimming. My little boy loves going there to swim with his friends whilst I enjoy watching the sailing. I like looking at water. But I don't really like getting wet!

As well as the lake, I love the town and its people too. My stepfather used to work in Lesotho where he met my Mam and myself. We used to visit Bala, his home town, every year and we fell in love with it, so at the end of the 1990s, we decided to settle here. Bala is quite similar to where I was brought up: it is surrounded by mountains and has a close-knit community. When I go shopping on Saturday, it takes me three hours because I'm talking to so many people! Everyone is really relaxed. We still have a lot of small shops that have been here for years. There was an attempt to build a Tesco store but the community was strongly against it for obvious reasons. That community spirit is one of the two things I appreciate most. The other is the Welsh language, which I have learned, and this has made a great difference, making it easier for me, both socially and at work. After all, over 80% of the population round Bala speak Welsh, so it's the everyday language.

The town and the lake, it's hard to imagine the one without the other. For me, they form one place and that place is my home.

Keneuoe Morgan

Tŷ Mawr, Ynys-y-Pandy

For me, one of the most impressive buildings within the Snowdonia National Park is the magnificent slate mill at Ynys-y-pandy. It rises above Afon Henwy, a gaunt, roofless but powerful ruin.

Industrial buildings, particularly those associated with the slate industry, tend to be plain and utilitarian – not so Tŷ Mawr! It has been likened to an abbey, a cathedral and a textile mill, but in fact it closely follows the conventional design for an iron foundry. It is one of the most remarkable industrial monuments in Wales, perhaps in Britain.

It was operational by 1857, processing slate slabs from the Gorseddau quarry into 'roofing slates, sawed and planed flooring-slabs, window sills, or slate slabs for general purposes.' The builder was a local man, Evan Jones of Garn Dolbenmaen, and though we do not know the name of the designer, we can hazard a guess. James Brunlees built the railway which connected the quarry and the mill to the sea. He had worked with Sir John Hawkshaw on the Manchester and Leeds Railway, and may well have been involved in building the railway works at Miles Platting, which centred on just such a building.

Archaeology has provided some clues as to how the mill worked. Power came from a water-wheel in the centre of the mill, and we know that there were circular saws and planing machines to shape the raw blocks, which arrived on rail wagons through the doorway in the southern wall. The first floor was probably given over to manufacturing ornamental-slate fireplace-surrounds, and these would have left on the ramped tramway.

Archaeology also confirms that the mill was a commercial flop! There is hardly any waste slate on the tips around the mill, proving that very little work ever went on here. It probably only worked for about eight years. Contemporaries agreed that the investors weren't fraudulent but they were naïve. There was everything there to make a success of the business except for workable slate. Plenty of engineering talent went into building and equipping Tŷ Mawr, but it would have been wise to have asked the opinion of a geologist – or better still, of an experienced Welsh quarryman.

It found re-use as a chapel around 1888 and an eisteddfod was even held in it. The machinery rusted away until 1894, when it was removed, and in 1906 the roof was taken off. In 1981, as a Scheduled Ancient Monument, it was purchased by the Snowdonia National Park and sympathetically consolidated – a memorial to the rash commercial optimism of the Victorian period.

David Gwyn

Last light, Ynys-y-pandy.

Llynnau Cregennen

Certain places have that special 'feel', that strange something you can't quite put your finger on. You arrive there for the first time in your life, and you suddenly feel elated, quietly excited. You never forget that feeling. Whenever you return, that same thrill surges through you. You're hooked. Llynnau Cregennen is that kind of place. We call them 'Llynnau Cregennen' around here, even though *llynnoedd* is the usual term for 'lakes'.

Some believe that the name comes from *cragen* which means 'shell', but others say that the original name was Crogenan because criminals would be hanged (*crogi*) here from a certain oak tree, after being sentenced in Llys Bradwen. This was the court of Ednywain ab Bradwen who lived here in the twelfth century, and apparently, the remains are still to be seen nearby – though I've never managed to find them.

I find it hard to believe that anybody could be killed here anyway, it's just too beautiful. But then again, you never know. It's eerily quiet here, dramatic and lonely in the shadow of Y Tyrrau Mawr and, come to think of it, I can't imagine a better place to die – in a quiet, contented sort of way at least. This is no place of suffering, it's more for romance and quiet contemplation – and falling in love. Call me a hopeless romantic, but it happened to me. Years ago, on a clear, balmy September night, I fell head over heels in love on the shores of Cregennen. He happened to be an easy man to fall for, but the location played a large part in my undoing. The sky was that perfect shade of dark blue no artist could ever reproduce on canvas, the stars were a brilliant kaleidoscope of crystals and the full moon shimmered on the silent waters. The little island looked almost Arthurian, I could almost see Excalibur rising from the mist, and I was completely gone.

There's a standing stone by the two lakes which proves that people have been passing this way for over four-thousand years, and I know – I feel it in my bones – that centuries of lovers have been compelled to stop here, as we did, and have been totally, completely spellbound.

Bethan Gwanas

Twilight at Llynnau Cregennen.

Foel Senigl

I farm 350 acres of land above Harlech and have lived there all my life. I've always liked going up Foel Senigl, a short distance above the farmhouse. It's the only place I know where there is such a good 360-degree view. On a clear day, you can see the Llŷn Peninsula; all the mountains in the Snowdon range; the estuaries of the Dwyryd and the Dwyfor; Cardigan Bay – and two castles, Harlech and Cricieth. Moving clockwise, you see a district that I feel should be in the National Park, namely Blaenau Ffestiniog. I enjoy pointing out that Snowdonia is the only National Park with a hole in the middle but I feel that the hole is very, very important because of its cultural heritage and as a tourist attraction. Further round, you come to the Rhinog range of mountains, the oldest gritstone, so they say, in the world. Carry on again and, if you are lucky, you can see the coastline of Pembrokeshire. It's fantastic scenery.

Nearer home, we have a lot of ancient monuments on the farm, including five standing stones. About a mile and a half from the farm are Muriau Gwyddelod or the Irishmen's huts, a series of round huts where Bronze-age settlers lived. There have been some successful archaeological digs on the land, which interested me a great deal. Shortly after one of these digs, we had just sprayed an area of land to eradicate bracken when I noticed, as I was going round the sheep one day, something which appeared to be a stone circle. It was one that Gresham hadn't found and it is now a registered ancient monument.

I remember going up Foel Senigl many years ago when the snow came in from the west. Everywhere the roads were blocked solid, and yet the summit of Snowdon was more or less clear of snow. It was bitterly cold and although it's only a thousand feet above sea level, I couldn't stay there long that day. It is very exposed and, like any area so at the mercy of the weather, it can be bleak and inhospitable.

But on a fine day, I don't think you could wish for more. I'm sure that the poet Eifion Wyn, were he alive today, wouldn't mind my appropriating his description of Cwm Pennant to my favourite place: '*Pam, Arglwydd, y gwnaethost Gwm Pennant mor dlws a bywyd hen fugail mor fyr?*' ('Why, Lord, did you make Cwm Pennant so lovely/And an old shepherd's life so short?'). It's the same spiritual feeling you have when you're up on Foel Senigl. On a still evening, which is when I best like to go up, you will hear the sounds of traffic. But when you look round the whole view and reach the Rhinogydd, they are completely unspoilt. Foel Senigl is something special.

Caerwyn Roberts

Summer evening, Foel Senigl.

ON SNOWDON'S BWLCH COCH

One of my most memorable experiences of Snowdonia was about twenty-five years ago, but is still vividly in my mind. A friend, Don Harris, and I were walking the Snowdon Horseshoe – one of the finest ridge-walks in Britain. Setting off from Pen y Pass, we left the Penygwryd track to begin the scramble up Crib Goch, and were soon in mist. On Crib Goch summit, the mist was thicker still and we could see only ten or twenty yards ahead. We had no sight of the precipitous drops on each side of the ridge. The rocks were dripping with water and so slippery that handholds as well as footholds were needed.

After the pinnacles, the ridge widens and a small descent brought us to Bwlch Coch, a comparatively flat, grassy area. We stopped to regain our breath before beginning the climb up to Garnedd Ugain, Snowdon's second peak. The cloud was beginning to lift. Areas of thinner mist swirled around us through which we could just discern some of the features below – before the mist thickened again. Parts of Llyn Llydaw and Glaslyn came momentarily into view, as did shadowy figures of walkers on the Miners' Track a thousand feet below.

As we stood looking down hoping for clearer views, we became aware of small windows opening in the cloud above. First to the east, the unmistakable profile of Moel Siabod with its green gentle slopes appeared in sunshine framed by swirling mist – just for a few seconds before the misty curtains closed again. Then the more jagged features of the Glyderau appeared, only to disappear rapidly again. As we watched, fascinated by these snapshots of the sunlit peaks to the east, we turned to see the same gradual process of disclosure occurring to the west. The impressive rock faces on Lliwedd began to appear – dark and threatening, no sun on them yet. The outline of Yr Wyddfa, the main Snowdon peak, could just be discerned although still deep in the mist. To the north, parts of Anglesey beyond the Menai Strait began to appear.

More windows were opening, some large, some small, all around us. The cloud was fighting to stay, the mountain battling to come through to show its beauty, the sun pressing to declare its glory. We stood transfixed for some twenty or thirty minutes until finally the sunshine won. Only Yr Wyddfa remained capped by cloud and that eventually cleared, too.

This gradual unveiling provided a more lasting impression of the beauty and grandeur of Snowdonia than had we seen it all at once. Creation can only truly be appreciated in small, even fleeting doses.

As a scientist, I have been exploring the marvellous workings of creation for most of my life. But the windows science opens, open only slowly and only show a small part at a time. There is only so much that our limited minds and emotions can appreciate at one time. So often, we 'see as through a glass darkly'. Don reminds me that when we finally left Bwlch Coch, I remarked 'I think heaven must be rather like that!'

SIR JOHN HOUGHTON

Crib Goch, with Moel Siabod beyond.

A Night by Llyn y Foel

Zipped up in a borrowed tent, satisfyingly full of a meal cooked on a borrowed stove. Nowhere else in the world I would want to be. At last, after half my life lived with a strong suspicion that I'm in the wrong place, I've come home to the mountains of Eryri, this time to stay forever.

Moel Siabod, for me, epitomises so much of what is special about the mountains of North Wales. A perfect little mountain; a wonderful viewpoint from which to gaze at so many other mountains; the first tempting peak to greet you as you approach Snowdonia along the A5, and with so many different ways to walk to the top, each one special. But I always walk up the same way, via Llyn y Foel.

Sleep eludes me, though I'm zipped up in my tent. I've been to the Himalayas and the Andes, but there's nowhere like this. At last I've come to Snowdonia to live and am spending some time in the hills. Just the hills and me. 'You can't take that old tent' said my friend Tom, 'take mine.'

First night out had to be Llyn y Foel. Up from Pont Cyfyng. Up across the moorland with Siabod rising invitingly in front, but I don't climb straight up. I like to turn left to walk past the little lake and then up past the quarry to Llyn y Foel. This path always reminds me of Middle Earth and somehow I wouldn't be surprised to bump into a band of hobbits and dwarves and men intent on their mission.

This was my first real mountain climb years earlier, with some friends who had done it all before. We stopped here, too, just to look at the Llyn, and the cwm and all those wonderful cliffs. And now, tucked up warm and cosy (Tom's tent is as old as mine, but definitely better!) I revel in the memories of those other times I've been here, basking in splendid isolation, or in the company of assorted friends, relatives and acquaintances who have come here with me.

Did I have a premonition then, on that first night by the Llyn, of all the future times I would come here? That in twenty years' time it would still be special? That one day my memories of this place would include the man who would be the father of my child, or include those nostalgic snatches of conversation as we enjoyed the lovely scrambly ridge from the Llyn to the summit? Or the day I first brought my son, who at eleven loved it just as much?

He loves it all: the sheer enjoyment of picking up on the mood of Middle Earth and bounding ahead, looking for the unexpected. Happily sleeping under the stars, waking up in the morning wet with dew. The satisfaction of achievement; getting there, finding the way, learning about sheep farming, seeing the world from the top, self-reliance. The pleasure of feeling at home, out on the hill. This must surely be the greatest gift I can give my child.

Jenny James

Drama at Llyn Y Foel.

Gwauncwmbrwynog

Ac wrth dy gyflwyno i Fab y Saer
Ac erfyn drosot, holaf yn daer
Beth a fyddi di, fy maban gwyn,
Wedi tyfu'n fawr ar y llethrau hyn?

Ai bugail defaid fel dy dad
A'r mynydd tawel iti'n stad?
Ynteu disgybl angau yn creu hafog
Yng Ngwauncwmbrwynog

R. Bryn Williams

Cwmbrwynog ('Valley of the Rushes') extends from the lower, grassy slopes of Llanberis up to the rugged crags of Clogwyn Coch and Clogwyn Du'r Arddu. It is steeped in history and tradition and has been commemorated in song and verse. The bleak, derelict remains of Hebron chapel stand proudly as a gateway to this magnificent valley. A bastion of history and past culture, it always seems to stand taller when shrouded in cloud but pales into insignificance in sunshine.

In the nineteenth and twentieth century, religion played a major part in the daily life of the Cwm. The first Sunday school was held at Nant Ddu Bach, a remote and windswept cottage, attended regularly by thirty-five children in 1825. Then, in 1831, sacrifices were made by the poor community of the Cwm to build the chapel and quench their religious thirst.

They say the old Welsh princes gathered on Moel Cynghorion ('the Mountain of Counsels') to plan battle against the might of Edward I. The conspicuous traces of nine medieval summer round-huts at the foot of Cynghorion are proof of the struggle that our forefathers endured to earn a meagre living. In the nineteenth and early twentieth century, copper and then slate miners left their scars on the mountain. The derelict slate mine below the Half Way Railway Bridge bears testimony to the harshness of unscrupulous early nineteenth-century landlords. After years of carving poor quality slate from the hillside, the workers were told to abandon their efforts without selling a single slate. The rows and rows of split and dressed slates, weather-beaten and moss-covered, are still there today, although hardly recognisable.

Industry and foolhardy men have caused much havoc and pollution in numerous forms. The noise of the early miners was soon overlaid by that of the Snowdon Mountain Railway constructed in the mid 1890s. This was the surreal brainchild of Lord Assheton-Smith of the Faenol estate, one of the richest aristocrats in the Principality. The railroad was probably just a gesture of one-upmanship. Then again, its constructor may have been a man ahead of his time. It is now one of Wales's major tourist attractions and an excellent source of employment for the new generation of Llanberis. I would miss the puffing and the panting of the hundred-year-old Swiss-made iron horses, especially since the present-day Hunslet diesel juggernauts hum a miserable tune. I am sure, however, that the lone voice of Reverend Canon H. O. Rawnsley from Barmouth, who objected to the construction of the railway in 1894, would have much more support in our time if another lord tried to plunder the valley in such a fashion.

The tranquillity of Cwmbrwynog was further disturbed during the Second World War when the British Army erected four ugly, concrete firing ranges across the lower valley. Some say that these eyesores should be dismantled but others argue that they should remain as a warning of the follies of man and his guns.

Ken Jones

Hebron chapel, Llanberis.

Llangelynnin Old Church

One day, nearly thirty years ago, I was exploring that shelf of high common grazing behind Conwy, when I came across an old church. Squat and grey, within a protective drystone wall, it seemed organic, as if it had grown out of its craggy surroundings. Undoubtedly, its stone would have been quarried locally, the oak for its roof timbers felled nearby. Between memorial stones, the grass was being mown by sheep rather than a machine. The interior was simplicity itself – some pews, a stone font, a lectern bearing a battered copy of Bishop Morgan's Bible, a decrepit organ and some faded inscriptions in Welsh on the wall behind the altar. Little else. I found myself moved by the bareness, the quietness and a powerful sense that this was a place, in T.S. Eliot's phrase, 'where prayer has been valid'.

What makes Eryri unique to me is the wealth of human history, from Neolithic *cromlech* to climbers' howff, to be found everywhere. Nowhere is this sense of human interaction with the landscape over countless generations more keenly felt than at Llangelynnin Old Church. Yet it is also a reminder of how depopulated these hills have become. Originally built in the thirteenth century, the church was enlarged in the fifteenth and sixteenth centuries to cater for an expanding community. Few live up here now. Dotted with ruined farms, this upland is probably emptier today than it has been for four thousand years. Stone circles, standing stones and sunken trackways bear witness to a prehistoric past when the climate was drier and warmer than it is now. Who knows but that the well in one corner of the churchyard may have been a place of healing in those Bronze-age times, or the dwelling of a Celtic deity. When Saint Celynnin arrived from Ireland, it would have made sense to establish himself close to a site already sacred. Only fifty yards from the well is a substantial hut-circle. It is obscured by tussock grass, but this could easily have been his original cell.

Today, the church is still in use. Often, there are freshly-cut flowers on the altar. One Sunday a month in summer, there is an afternoon service. It is usually well attended, with walking boots and wellies much in evidence along with dogs lying at their mistresses' feet. Sunlight streams through the open door and, in quiet moments, a blackbird can be heard outside. It feels right. In the Celtic church, Man was still very much a part of nature. For the rest of the time, the visitors' book reveals that I am not alone in being affected by the place, without need of liturgy or ritual. A 'still, small voice of calm' can be heard, too often drowned out in hurried, unmindful lives. Maybe what we feel is in essence what made the well holy long long ago, something mysterious and unknowable, but present for all that.

Rob Collister

Sanctuary, Llangelynnin Church.

LLYN GLAS ISLAND

A tiny island in one of Snowdonia's smallest lakes. A small mountain oasis discreetly located below the imposing dark cliffs of Crib Goch and Clogwyn y Person, high above Dyffryn Peris.

Springtime sees the island inaccessible by sheep; fresh and green, blossoming with yellow flowers, standing out from the surrounding barren, over-grazed landscape.

A solitary tree, windswept, a sanctuary for mountain birds.

But often, during harsh Winter months, the lake is solid, its ripples frozen in time, as if a Northern Witch has waved her wand in anger casting a momentary spell...

For those who know of its existence and location, it is a welcome sight, almost like an old friend, when descending carefully through mountain mists or windy snow, from the furthest desolate corners of Cwm Glas or from the heights of Bwlch Coch back down to the safety and comfort of lower ground, and home.

A refuge, a haven – a temporary escape from the fragile reality of everyday life to an enduring tenuous existence in the mountains.

NIKKI WALLIS

Arthurian twilight, Llyn Glas.

NOTES ON CONTRIBUTORS

Sir Kyffin Williams (p. 12-13)

Born in Llangefni, Anglesey in 1918, Kyffin Williams R.A. has achieved international recognition as an artist with a highly distinctive style. A diagnosis of epilepsy in 1941 halted his army career in the Royal Welch Fusiliers, after which he took up painting, studying at the Slade School of Fine Art, London and subsequently combined painting with teaching art at Highgate School for many years, returning to Wales in 1974. He has received many honours including a D.Litt from the University of Wales, the Medal of the Honourable Society of Cymmrodorion, the Glyndŵr Medal and the Medal of the Contemporary Art Society of Wales. He is President of the Royal Cambrian Academy and is Deputy Lieutenant for Gwynedd.

Iolo Williams (p. 14-15)

Born in Builth Wells, Iolo Williams spent most of his childhood in Llanwddyn (Lake Vyrnwy). After taking an ecology degree, he worked for a short time in farming and forestry before joining the staff of the RSPB in mid-Wales. Frequently asked to contribute to radio and television, he left the RSPB after fourteen-and-a-half years to work in the media full-time. Since then he has become well known as a TV presenter in both English and Welsh-language series including *Wild Wales*, *Wild Winter*, *Special Reserves*, *A Natural History of Wales, Crwydro* and *Teithiau Tramor Iolo*. He is married with two sons.

Sian Roberts (p. 16-17)

Having spent her childhood playing in and around Penrhyndeudraeth, Afon Dwyryd and the surrounding hills, Sian Roberts 'proceeded to spend the rest of [her] adult life playing in the rest of Snowdonia'. After a few years of fell running, she moved on to mountain-bike racing and travelled all over the world competing for team GB. As a means of earning a living, Siôn Parry, Dafydd (her husband) and Sian set up Beics Betws in Betws-y-coed. She and Dafydd then moved on to develop Coed-y-Brenin into the renowned mountain-biking centre it now is.

Dafydd Iwan (p. 18-19)

Dafydd Iwan was born in Brynaman in 1943, moving to Llanuwchllyn where his father was the local minister in 1955. After Ysgol Tan Domen in Bala, he studied at University College Aberystwyth and the Welsh School of Architecture, Cardiff. He was Chairman of the Welsh Language Society between 1968-71 and was imprisoned more than once for participating in its campaigns. Since 2003 he has been President and Leader of Plaid Cymru. He has been a prominent composer and singer and is a Director of Sain, a company employing forty people in the Caernarfon area. He is married to Bethan and they have two sons. He also has three children from his first marriage.

Lord Dafydd Elis Thomas (p. 20-21)

Lord Dafydd Elis Thomas is the Presiding Officer of the First National Assembly for Wales. A former university lecturer, he was made a Life Peer in 1992 having served as the MP for Meirionnydd 1974-1983 and Meirionnydd Nant Conwy 1983-1992. He was Chair of the Welsh Language Board 1994-1999, and a member of the Welsh Arts Council and the British Film Institute. He was Chair of Screen 1992-99 and a former director and Vice-chair of Cynefin Environmental Ltd over the same period. He is a member of the Governing Body of the Church in Wales and has been the President of Bangor University since 2000.

Louise Thomas (p. 22-23)

Louise Thomas is the Chief Instructor at Plas y Brenin, the National Mountain Centre and the British Mountaineering Club Vice-president. She originally trained as a teacher but is now qualified as an International Mountain Guide and Mountain Instructor. She is a 'super keen' climber with extensive experience throughout the UK and the Alps. She has been on a wide variety of big-wall trips abroad, making first ascents in Jordan, Patagonia, Pakistan, Borneo, Greenland, Baffin Island, Norway, Madagascar and Mali, as well as climbing classic routes in Yosemite and Colorado.

Ieuan Wyn (p. 24-25)

Ieuan Wyn was born in Dyffryn Ogwen in 1949. He received his primary and secondary education in the area, and after qualifying as a teacher at Coleg Normal, Bangor he taught in primary schools in Aberaeron, Llandudno, Tregarth and Llanrug. He retired from teaching in 2004. He is married to Blodeuwedd, and they have a daughter and two sons. He won the Chair at the National Eisteddfod of Wales in 1987, and he has published a volume of verse entitled *Llanw a Thrai*. He is co-editor of Y *Faner Newydd*, a national quarterly, and Secretary of Cylch yr Iaith.

Barbara Jones (p. 26-27)

Barbara Jones has had a lifelong interest in many aspects of mountains, including their geomorphology, ecology and vegetation and has spent many a happy hour exploring, climbing and walking in Snowdonia, as well as in several other mountain ranges of the world. Since 1985, she has worked for the Nature Conservancy Council and Countryside Council for Wales (CCW) in Scotland and in North Wales and is currently CCW's Upland Ecologist for Wales. Recent research into the ecology, genetics and conservation of the Snowdon Lily has further developed her interest and specialism in arctic-alpine, cliff and montane flora.

Jane Pullee (p. 28-29)

Born in Prestwich, Jane Pullee was four years old when her parents bought the Pen-y-Gwryd Hotel, Nant Gwynant. It proved a highly successful venture, achieving fame as the Snowdonia training-base for the 1953 Everest team. Leaving home, she attended secretarial college in London and then became a personal assistant to William Donaldson, an impressario of *Beyond the Fringe* fame. Later she worked for BOAC for ten years, first as a stewardess and then in the marketing department. However, when her parents decided they might sell Pen-y-Gwryd, she knew she had to return to Wales. With her father initally, she and her husband, Brian, have run the Pen-y-Gwryd since 1975. They have two sons.

Ronwen Roberts (p. 30-31)

Ronwen Roberts was born in 1954 and was brought up in Blaenau Ffestiniog where she now works for Women's Aid. In 1969 at Ysgol y Moelwyn comprehensive, geography teacher Del Davies formed a walking/climbing club which met regularly. Del inspired Ronwen and other students to explore climbing and walking, both locally and in other wild places in Snowdonia. A founder member of Grŵp Gwarchod Rhosydd (a pressure group formed to challenge quarrying in the Moelwynion), she has also served on the Executive Committee of the Snowdonia Society. Along with other local people, she is currently forming a walking/outdoor club for young people in Blaenau Ffestiniog.

Kim Burnham (p. 32-33)

Kim Burnham joined the Forestry Commission in 1987 and is now the Eryri and Ynys Môn Area Manager. He was born in Stamford, Lincolnshire. In 1982 he moved to Bangor to take a degree in Agriculture and Forestry. He has stayed in Wales since then, apart from the three years he spent working in Nepal for the Community Forest Regeneration Programme. He is a member of the Ogwen Valley Mountain Rescue Team. He lives with his wife and two boys in the middle of the Forest above Betws-y-coed and spends his time in the forest or climbing.

Kathryn Davies (p. 34-35)

Kathryn Davies was born on a hill farm in Staylittle, near Llanidloes in Powys. After boarding school at Dr Williams's School in Dolgellau she did a pre-nursing course at a technical college in Newtown, Powys and nurse training (general) at the Royal Shrewsbury Hospital. She met her husband at the Young Farmers' Movement, married in 1985 and has two children. At present her job is helping both indoors with the housework and outdoors on the farm, especially with the stock. For a number of years she has been a judge of the Snowdonia Society's biennial Farming and Landscape Award.

Anne Lloyd-Jones (p. 36-37)

Anne Lloyd-Jones was born in the Dysynni Valley in 1951 and educated in Bryncrug, Oswestry, Dolgellau and London, before returning to Wales in 1972. She runs a farm-tourism business and has been Chairman of Mid Wales Tourism since 2001. Also active in local politics, she is a member (and past Mayor) of Tywyn Council and a Gwynedd County Councillor. She is founder member and Vice-chairman of Gwynedd Economic Partnership and a member of the Snowdonia National Park CAE panel, and is involved in many charitable organisations in the area. She and her husband John (Chairman of CCW) have three daughters.

Merfyn Williams (p. 38-39)

Merfyn Williams became the Executive Director of Cynnal Cymru, the Sustainable Development Forum for Wales in 2003, following nine years as Director of the Campaign for the Protection of Rural Wales (CPRW). Earlier posts include Principal of the Snowdonia National Park Study Centre at Plas Tan-y-Bwlch, Senior Lecturer in Environmental Issues at Coleg Normal, Bangor, and Director of the Postgraduate Diploma in Countryside Management. He has written about Industrial Archaeology and Countryside Conservation and is author of the Official Guide to Snowdonia (2002). Living in Croesor, he is a trustee of the Portmeirion Foundation and first Chairman of Menter Llanfrothen, a village association which acquired the village shop and rebuilt it on ecological principles.

Gwyn Thomas (p. 40-41)

Gwyn Thomas has been farming Blaen-y-Nant, Nant Ffrancon since 1996. He was born and brought up above Gerlan. After studying at Glynllifon Agricultural College, near Caernarfon, he spent eight years employed on different types of farm before deciding that shepherding suited him best. He was a shepherd in Dolawen, Nant Ffrancon, for thirteen years and then became self-employed, working with sheep and cattle. During this time he was very much involved with Blaen-y-Nant and grew to love the area. He believes strongly in farming in a way that cares for the environment. Blaen-y-Nant is now well known for its organic beef and lamb and also for the welcome extended to the public and to school groups.

Warren Martin (p.42-43)

Warren Martin was brought up in Llanfairfechan. After Army service in the Far East, he served in the Colonial Police in Kenya (where he was a founder member of the Kenya Wildlife Society). In 1962 he became first Head Warden of the Caernarfonshire section of the Snowdonia National Park. He joined the Nature Conservancy as a Reserve Warden in 1966, becoming Chief Warden in 1971. He remained in that post through the changes from Nature Conservancy to Countryside Council for Wales, retiring in 1995. He became an appointed member of the Snowdonia National Park Authority in 1997 and is currently the Vice-chairman. He is a Vice-president of the Snowdonia Society.

David Nash (p. 44-45)

David Nash was born in 1945 in the south of England. His grandparents lived in Llan Ffestiniog and consequently much of his childhood was spent in this mountainous region. After art college, he moved to Blaenau Ffestiniog where, over forty years, he has established his studios and an international reputation as a sculptor working mainly in wood. His work is in major public collections including the National Museum of Wales, the Tate Gallery, London, and the Guggenheim Museum, New York. In 1999 he was elected Royal Academician and received an O.B.E. for services to Art in 2004.

Jim Perrin (p.46-47)

Of Welsh descent, Jim Perrin was brought up in post-war, inner-city Manchester, and from the age of twelve wandered off into the hills at every opportunity. From the age of seventeen he has lived in Wales, having his romantic notions of an undespoiled landscape and a cultured, egalitarian and meritocratic society ground away by the everyday, the contingent and the modern. After working as a shepherd in Cwm Pennant, he began to make his living from writing, and now, decades on, lives reclusively among the moors, observes human ambition with a kind of saddened glee, but still finds the natural world redemptive and overwhelmingly worthy of celebration.

Owen Wyn Owen (p. 48-49)

Owen Wyn Owen was born at Pont Cyfyng, Capel Curig in 1925. In 1943 he started his army training with a two-year engineering course followed by an officer cadetship. After an accident he was discharged in 1947. He then obtained a London University Engineering Degree and worked as a lecturer at Bangor Technical College, where he became Deputy Head of Engineering. He has been a local councillor for fifty years. Now retired, he pursues his lifelong interest in vintage cars, which has included the restoration to running order of Parry Thomas's land-speed-record car 'Babs', buried in the Pendine sand dunes for 42 years.

Geoff Elliott (p. 50-51)

Geoff Elliott was a former Vice-chairman and member of the Snowdonia Society's Executive Committee. He was also a member of CPRW and of the Ramblers' Association, and was a voluntary Snowdonia National Park Warden. Born, and spending his working life in Cardiff, he moved to Dolgellau after retirement, and later to Harlech. He considered that Meirionnydd offers some of the finest walking in Wales, and he wrote two books of walks to help people explore the area, one of walks around Dolgellau, and the other around Harlech.

(Sadly, Geoff Elliott died in March 2005)

Sarah Jones (p. 52-53)

A farmer's daughter, from Ganllwyd, near Dolgellau, Sarah Jones works for the Environment Agency. After studying Woodland and Environmental Studies (Coleg Meirion Dwyfor), and Countryside Management (Aberystwyth University), she has worked for many conservation organisations. Her first posts were Lake Warden on Llyn Tegid, Bala, for the Snowdonia National Park Authority and receptionist at the Snowdonia Society's Ugly House. Then she joined the North Wales Wildlife Trust working as a People and Wildlife Officer at Gwaith Powdwr, Porthmadog, the old Cook's explosive factory, now a superb nature reserve. However, her favourite job of all was presenting wildlife programmes for S4C, from South Africa, Sri Lanka, Mexico and Canada, all in one year!

Keneuoe Morgan (p. 54-55)

Keneuoe Morgan is the Development Officer, Antur Penllyn, a community regeneration enterprise based in Bala. Married with a six-year-old son, she has lived in Bala since she was nineteen years old when she came to the UK from Lesotho. She is a Bala Town Councillor. Keen on sports, she has undertaken netball training for children as a volunteer and was a children's athletics trainer in the past. In 2000 she won the Dafydd Orwig Memorial Prize for Welsh learners in Gwynedd and also reached the final round of the 'Welsh Learner of the Year' competition at the National Eisteddfod. She is now a fluent Welsh speaker.

David Gwyn (p. 56-57)

David Gwyn was born in Bangor and spent his early childhood in the industrial town of Bethesda at the foot of the great Penrhyn slate quarries. Although he moved to England as a child, he never lost his fascination with the landscape of Snowdonia nor with the remains of the industries which once sustained a unique and living Welsh culture – its slate quarries, its copper mines and textile mills. He now works as an independent archaeological consultant, teaches part-time in the Division of Heritage Management at the University of Wales, Bangor and edits *Industrial Archaeology Review*.

Bethan Gwanas (p. 58-59)

Bethan Gwanas was born and bred in Dolgellau. She has been an English teacher with VSO in Nigeria, a radio producer, French and outdoor-activities teacher and Deputy Manager of Glan-llyn – but is now a full-time author. Her first novel *Amdani!* was adapted for both television and the stage, and she has won the Tir na n-Og award twice. She has also written numerous plays for children for Cwmni'r Frân Wen and the BBC (Welsh and English). She enjoys travelling and in 2003, she presented *Ar y Lein*, a TV series following latitude 52 around the world, which was followed by another trip along a longitude line via the North and South Poles in 2004/5.

Caerwyn Roberts (p. 60-61)

Caerwyn Roberts is a Merionnydd farmer, the third generation of his family on the holding. He has been Chair of the Snowdonia National Park Authority since 1999, is a past Chair of the Association of National Park Authorities (UK) and is presently Vice-Chair. He has been a J.P. since 1988. He won the Daily Telegraph Farming Excellence Award 2003 (NFU England and Wales) for his valuable contribution to farming and the environment. He was one of the first farmers to encourage school groups to visit his farm and has a regular programme of school visits.

Sir John Houghton (p. 62-63)

John Houghton was born in Dyserth, Clwyd and educated at Rhyl Grammar School and Jesus College, Oxford. During his career as a scientist, he has been Professor of Atmospheric Physics at Oxford University, Chief Executive of the Meteorological Office, Chairman of the Royal Commission on Environmental Pollution and Chairman of the Scientific Assessment for the Intergovernmental Panel on Climate Change. His many awards include gold medals from the Royal Astronomical Society and the Royal Meteorological Society and an honorary doctorate from the University of Wales. His books include *Global Warming: the Complete Briefing* and *The Search for God: can science help?*. He now lives in Aberdyfi where he enjoys sailing and mountain walking.

Jenny James (p. 64-65)

Jenny James first came to Snowdonia on holiday with her parents in the 1960s and decided that this is where she wanted to be. She later worked on a farm near Beddgelert before studying agriculture at the Welsh Agricultural College in Aberystwyth. In 1985 she returned to live in Snowdonia and since then has worked on a wide variety of environmental issues through her employment and voluntary work with the National Trust, the Snowdonia Society, Friends of the Earth and the very successful A5 Consortium. She currently lives on a smallholding at the foot of Snowdon with her son Harry.

Ken Jones (p. 66-67)

Ken Jones is a retired Civil Servant born and brought up in Llanberis. A founder member of the Eryri Harriers Running Club, he is the founder and organiser of the International Snowdon Race from 1976 to date. He is Secretary of the local committee that was instrumental in establishing a twinning link between Llanberis and Morbegno in northern Italy, finalised in October 2004. This followed participation in the Snowdon Race by runners from this city for 25 years. A kidney-transplant patient himself, he is also Secretary of the Ysbyty Gwynedd Kidney Patients' Association. He is a keen conservationist and local historian.

Rob Collister (p. 68-69)

Rob Collister is a qualified mountain guide whose work takes him all over the world, climbing and ski-mountaineering. His three children were born and brought up in Glasgwm, Penmachno but he and his wife, Netti, now live at the lower end of the Conwy valley, near Henryd. He is the author of *Lightweight Expeditions* (Crowood Press 1989) and *Over the Hills and Far Away* (Ernest Press 1996) and writes frequently for outdoor magazines and journals.

Nikki Wallis (p. 70-71)

Nikki Wallis comes from Llanberis. She has worked as a National Park Warden since 1999 dealing with recreational-access issues and sustainable enjoyment of the fragile mountain environment. Following an honours degree in Biochemistry and Molecular Biology (University of Wales, Bangor), she has gained a postgraduate diploma / MA in Countryside Management. She is an active member of the Alpine Club (London) and the Swiss Alpine Club, having climbed mountains extensively all around the world since childhood. She is also an active member of the Llanberis Mountain Rescue Team and has two mountain-rescue-search dogs. She runs a non-profit international organisation, Mountains for Active Diabetics.

Notes on Poems

p.52
This verse evokes the sustenance that this seemingly bleak stretch of land offers the poet, and how its ancient history is revealed season by season.

p.66
This extract, from a poem that celebrates a child's baptism, ponders whether the young boy will grow up to be a shepherd, like his father, or one who will be a scourge to the valley.

The Challenge of Eryri

We shall not cease from exploration
and the end of all our exploring
will be to arrive where we started
and know the place for the first time.

T.S. Eliot 'Little Gidding', *Four Quartets*

The contributors to this book were set a difficult task, because selecting only one favourite location in Eryri would seem an impossible choice. I considered the question on many occasions, usually when sitting beside the camera; maybe during the pre-dawn chill of a winter's day or the twilight warmth of a summer's evening, waiting for the light, or, more likely, for the rain to stop! For as wonderful and evocative as Eryri's scenery is, its ever-changing moods provide a real challenge for the landscape photographer.

But then Eryri does not let you into its affections easily. Its capricious nature accompanies a soft splendour, a quiet grandeur that isn't waved in your face at every turn. This understated beauty makes good compositions, and hence good images, difficult to realise, and it demands that you look longer and harder, both into Eryri and into yourself.

Over the years we've come to an understanding. If I put in enough effort then, like a coy lover, Eryri will show her appreciation of my attentions by whispering a secret, and allow me to see something truly magical. Then the miles of walking and the hours of waiting are forgotten, and it's the few moments of enchantment that are remembered, and treasured.

And my favourite location in Eryri? I'm often asked a similar question about my images: which is my favourite? My answer's always the same: 'it's the one I see tomorrow.' The same could be said about my favourite location.

Creating the images for this book has been hard work, hugely enjoyable and immensely satisfying, all in equal measure. It could not have been achieved though without support from many others, so whilst echoing the acknowledgements made at the beginning of the book, I would like to say a particular thank you to the following:

the members of the Snowdonia Society for their continuing enthusiasm for my work;
Ceri and all at Gomer Publishing for the opportunity;
Nathan Wake at Fujifilm for his support and advice;
my family and friends for understanding my absences.

My warmest thanks are reserved for you Heather, for your patience, understanding, enthusiasm and unstinting support. Yours is the truest light in my life.

Steve Lewis

THE TECHNICAL BIT

Landscape photography makes big demands of camera equipment. It is pushed and pulled in and out of rucksacks; subjected to extremes of temperature and weather; it has to be light, strong and reliable. The most important consideration, however, is that the camera should complement the photographer's working methods and aesthetic needs. The equipment should never hinder the creative process.

All the images in this book were made using an Ebony RW45 large format (LF) folding field camera, using 65mm, 90mm, 150mm, 210mm and 270mm lenses from Schneider, Rodenstock and Nikon. I metered using a Sekonic L508 spot meter. To many, this system appears old-fashioned and awkward (the design is little changed in a hundred years), but to get the best from it demands a disciplined, measured approach. Combined with the philosophy behind the design and use of LF cameras, this perfectly suits the way I approach my photography. With a large-format camera you don't take photographs; you make photographs.

Film doesn't 'see' light the way we do, so filters are often necessary to balance exposure and colour. I carry a large selection of filters, all manufactured by Lee filters in Andover. This includes the 81 series of warming filters, 0.3, 0.6 and 0.9 graduated neutral density (GND) filters with both hard and soft gradations, and a polariser. I also have a couple of 'specials', which combine an 81C filter with a GND filter.

The film stock used throughout was Fuji Provia 100F transparency film, which I have used since its introduction. I find Provia very natural in its colour and contrast, and very forgiving with the long exposures often required in landscape work. It is loaded using Fuji's Quickload system, which, although more expensive than traditional holders, is smaller and lighter, and negates the problems of dust and dirt. The panoramic format shots were taken on Fuji Provia 100F transparency roll film loaded into a 6 x12 back.

Like most photographers I have a love-hate relationship with tripods. They have to be sturdy enough to keep the camera steady, but light enough to carry long distances. Modern materials, such as carbon fibre, go some way towards reconciling these contradictory requirements, but I have yet to find the perfect tripod; so I have two! My aluminium Gitzo Explorer is very stable and versatile, but weighs a hefty 3.7kgs, and is reserved for short trips. My Velbon Sherpa Pro is marginally less versatile, but weighs only 2.2kgs. and is used on longer trips and overnight stays. Both tripods are fitted with a Manfrotto 410 geared head, which allows for precise framing.

Whilst some locations are a few minutes from the car, I often trek to remote locations, spending many hours out, often at unsociable times. At these times it's necessary to carry all the paraphernalia needed to explore the landscape safely. This includes map, compass, GPS unit, waterproofs, first-aid kit, food, fluids, torch, spare clothing etc. Overnight stays require a sleeping bag, bivvy bag, and a stove.

All the equipment (except the tripod) is carried in a Lowepro Super Trekker rucksack, which has an average loaded weight of approximately 18kgs.

STEVE LEWIS

FIELD NOTES ON THE 30 PRIVATE VIEWS OF SNOWDONIA

These notes have been transcribed from my field book. Space means they are brief, but they are offered in the hope they will provide some insight.

Winter solstice sunrise, Crib Goch.   **p. 13**

This light spectacular was my reward for an early start and an hour's walk in −15°C temperatures. For 15 minutes either side of sunrise, the light just got better and better. Then the clouds and a blizzard rolled in, and I retreated to the car, cold and tired, but elated.

Craig Goch and the Migneint.   **p. 15**

At first glance featureless, the Migneint is a treasure trove for anyone prepared to pull on a pair of walking boots. The acidic soil conditions allow heather and mosses to flourish, and I composed this image, with a heather-covered rock outcrop and Craig Goch as a backdrop, to give a flavour of the area.

Afon Dwyryd and the Moelwynion.   **p. 17**

This viewpoint took a little scouting because as well as Afon Dwyryd with the Moelwynion as a backdrop, I wanted to include Gelli Grin quay mentioned by Sian in the text. The visit was timed for an ebb tide, and the resulting sandbank has provided a shapely foreground. Despite using a long lens, the shot retains a good feeling of depth.

Llanuwchllyn station.   **p. 19**

The staff at Llanuwchllyn station are superb, and nothing was too much trouble – even when I positioned my camera on the track! Drop front on the camera has allowed inclusion of the track signal whilst keeping the camera back vertical to retain a proper shape in the buildings.

Industrial relics, Trawsfynydd.
I was so keen to have this slate bridge as a foreground that I finished up balanced precariously on a crumbling abutment. Despite their both being relics of the past, the resulting juxtaposition of old and new industries couldn't be more stark, both compositionally and figuratively.

Stormy day, Nant Peris.
I climbed to this spot on three occasions, and each time the weather was awful. In the absence of any quality light, I explored the shapes in the rocks and the valley beyond, and endeavoured to portray a typical December day in Snowdonia.

Yr Elen and Afon Llafar.
Snow can present exposure challenges, but a manual spot meter enabled me to balance the exposure with a GND filter, thereby preserving detail in both the reflection and the sunlit peak. Because of the blue skies, the snow would have had a strong blue tint, so an 81D filter was used to reinstate what we perceive as being the correct hue.

The Snowdon Lily (*Lloydia serotina*).
Lloydia has a precarious existence, the nooks and crannies it inhabits being amongst the most inhospitable and inaccessible in Snowdonia. I framed the tiny flower against the cold, hard rocks and the roseroot (*Sedum rosea*) and, not wanting to tint the delicate hue in the petals, left the shot unfiltered. The resulting cool tone has added to the overall impression of fragile life flourishing in an unforgiving environment.

Afon Gwryd and the Glyderau. p. 29

Fortunately this spot is not too far from the road, as four visits were needed before the right combination of water and light came together. After checking with the spot meter, I decided against using a GND, as it would have toned down the splash of light on the Glyderau, ruining a small but important part of the mood.

On the yellow line, the Moelwynion. p. 31

I wanted to make a photograph standing on the yellow line Ronwen mentions in her essay. Strange to think that a few metres either side of this spot places you inside or outside the National Park, with all that implies. The landscape, however, doesn't care about lines on a map, and it was wonderful whichever way I looked.

Autumn light in the Gwydyr, Moel Siabod beyond. p. 33

The area around Llyn Elsi gives fine views over the Gwydyr forest in all directions, and it's a favourite haunt of mine. I'm always spoilt for choice, but I couldn't resist the backlighting on these trees, which is further enhanced by the dark clouds over Siabod.

Fron Oleu, the Moelwynion beyond. p. 34-35

Kathryn's farm (bottom right) is surrounded by stunning scenery, but in the valley I couldn't find a composition that did the location justice. So I climbed an adjacent hill, and looked back towards the Moelwynion and Cnicht. I just had time to expose my film before the shadows overwhelmed the farm.

Fault line, the Dysynni valley. p. 37

The Dysynni valley is part of an old geological fault that runs southwest to northeast through Snowdonia. This viewpoint was chosen to show its varied contours, moulded by the ancient forces of nature, and its landscape, created by the modern hand of man.

Cwm Croesor and the coast from Cnicht. p. 39

Vista-type compositions can be difficult to resolve, as often the resulting image fails to capture the grandeur of the scene. Keen to get a view to the coast, I was up and down Cnicht a few times before I found this outcrop to act as a foreground. It helps create depth in the image, and adds to the alternating highlight and shadow design.

Summer evening, Nant Ffrancon. p. 41

Although one of Snowdonia's busiest areas, by late evening the climbers and walkers have retired to the pubs, and you can have Nant Ffrancon to yourself. The foreground waterfall starts a curve of highlights, bordered by shadow areas, which lead the eye through the picture space. Gwyn's farmhouse can be seen on the left.

Llyn Anafon and Llwytmor from Pen Bryn-du. p. 43

As a photographer, I'm not fond of clear skies. They tend to be bland and give images a cool feel, especially in the shadow areas. However, on this afternoon there were a few clouds about, and so I waited for some to drift into the right place. Heather served up a picnic, and we soaked up the late afternoon sun whilst cloud-watching.

Touchstone, Afon Cynfal.   p. 45

An eternal Methuselah, the rock appears to be resisting both the advancing woodlands and at the same time the river's attempts to draw it away into the depths. Timeless poise in a constantly shifting environment.

Spring in Cwm Pennant.   p. 47

Arriving late one May afternoon, I was surprised to find the valley swathed in bluebells. Strong sunlight is not ideal for photographing the delicate flowers, but how could I resist this scene? Drop front on the camera was used to fill the foreground with flowers, keeping the uninspiring sky to a minimum.

Flowing shapes and stepping stones, Afon Llugwy.   p. 49

I was keen to photograph the stepping stones mentioned by Owen, but couldn't resist echoes of the flowing river in these grasses. Despite the wide aperture dictated by the gloomy light (and a constant drizzle), a little tilt on the front standard has kept everything sharp. I spent an hour standing in the river, but light relief was provided by a group of canoeists who treated me as just another obstacle on their way down stream!

Clearing storm, Gloywlyn.   p. 51

The forecast had promised improving weather, and for an hour before sunset, it was on the cusp; a mix of sun and storm on a huge stage; Snowdonia as drama queen. All that's required of the photographer in these instances is to capture the light as it's splashed on the landscape.

Sunrise, Ffridd Bryn Coch farm.   p. 53

Sarah took me up to this spot and asked 'Can I have the view from here please?' Who was I to refuse? I calculated that dawn would be the best time, and half an hour after sunrise the right combination of light, shadows and mist came together. Ffridd Bryn Coch can be seen in the middle distance.

Spring morning, Llyn Tegid.   p. 55

At sunrise on this spring morning, Llyn Tegid was calm and serene. In these situations the tranquillity of the scene is best served with a simple, uncluttered composition. The stones and Aran Fawddwy combine to form a pleasing 'S' shape in the frame.

Last light, Ynys-y-pandy.   p. 57

Ynys-y-pandy is nearly always photographed from the front. Looking for something different, I found this composition amongst the slate tips at the rear, although it took six visits before I got the light I was looking for. The shot required compound movements on the camera, which not only tested its versatility, but also my patience!

Twilight at Llynnau Cregennen.   p. 59

After hours of persistent rain, I was rewarded with half an hour of magic. The understated, soft light in this image works well; strong, dramatic lighting would have ruined the calm feeling. A quiet end to a stormy day – and promising a better day tomorrow.

Summer evening, Foel Senigl.   p. 61

The views from Senigl in all directions are stunning, and there's an abundance of riches for the photographer. I chose a view down the coast, with the summit cairn picked out by the late evening light. The bench invites you to sit and soak up the warm remnants of the day.

Crib Goch, with Moel Siabod beyond.   p. 63

Having visited Bwlch Y Moch (bottom right) without finding a satisfactory composition, I climbed towards Garnedd Ugain, eventually looking back to see this scene. Constantly-changing light meant picking my moment before tripping the shutter, although I was kept entertained during the wait, bantering with walkers as they squeezed past my tripod on the narrow ridge!

Drama at Llyn Y Foel.   p. 65

In cahoots with a stiff breeze, the sun was playing hide-and-seek with the clouds. Exposing for the highlights has added to the drama, but only two of the six sheets of film exposed were sharp. In anything above a fresh breeze, large format cameras have the characteristics of a box kite!

Hebron chapel, Llanberis.   p. 67

I've always been intrigued by the way the landscape reclaims the works of man once they're abandoned. This composition explores the chapel's return to the tones and textures of the rocks that lie around it, and from which it originated. Keeping the camera back vertical has ensured a proper shape in the chapel, whilst a small amount of tilt on the front standard has ensured sharpness right through the image.

Sanctuary, Llangelynnin Church.   p. 69

Fortunately Llangelynnin's white painted walls evened out the light levels, keeping the contrast within the film's capabilities. With the weather on the bad side of foul, I made my images to the sound of the wind howling around the eaves and rain beating at the windows. But, as it has since the thirteenth century, Llangelynnin afforded a tranquil space.

Arthurian twilight, Llyn Glas.   p. 71

Nestling below Crib Goch, and with fine views down Nant Peris and to the Glyderau, Llyn Glas is a wonderfully atmospheric place. Legend has it that Merlin hid the throne of England here when the Saxons invaded. Certainly, sitting on the shore at twilight, it's easy to imagine the Lady of the Lake rising from its waters, wielding Excalibur.

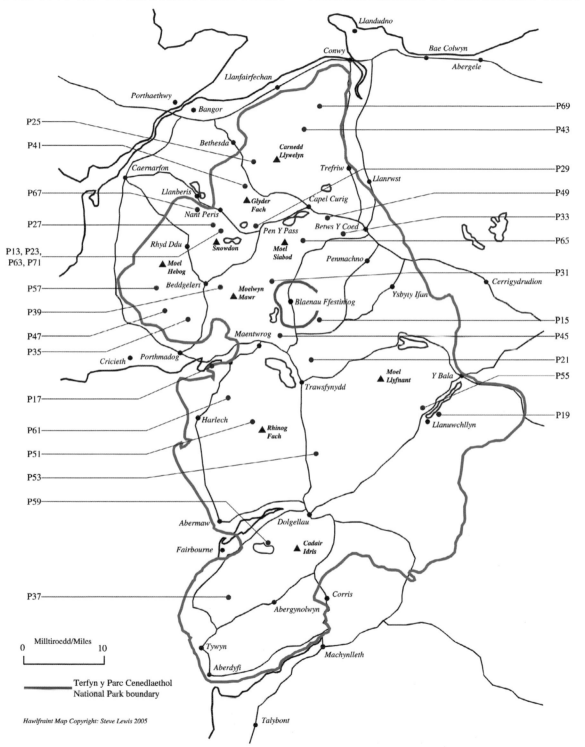

THE SNOWDONIA SOCIETY

The Snowdonia Society, founded in 1967, works to ensure that the beauty and diversity of the Snowdonia National Park landscape, wildlife and culture remain for present and future generations to enjoy. With over 2,500 members, it is the foremost charity working to protect and enhance the National Park.

The Society is particularly active in:

> monitoring development proposals in the National Park, taking appropriate action if thought necessary; for example, it opposes the proliferation of wind turbines just outside the Park boundaries and the siting of mobile-phone masts in prominent sites within the Park;
>
> studying and commenting critically on any policy papers or consultations affecting the Park;
>
> organising clear-up of litter and fly-tipping, footpath restoration, removal of invasive species, especially rhododendron and other similar initiatives;
>
> running an annual drystone-walling competition and biennial Farming and Landscape Awards to encourage traditional skills and environmentally sensitive farming;
>
> providing a programme of walks and talks for members, who also receive the twice-yearly magazine and an autumn newsletter.

The Society works closely with local communities and other organisations with similar aims such as the Snowdonia National Park Authority, Countryside Council for Wales, the Campaign for the Protection of Rural Wales, Keep Wales Tidy, Gwynedd and Conwy County Councils.

A substantial part of the Society's funding comes from members' subscriptions but the Society also receives grants, and sponsorship for specific activities from a range of organisations including statutory bodies, charitable trusts and corporate bodies.

Since 1988, the Snowdonia Society has been based in Tŷ Hyll ('the Ugly House'), Capel Curig, a striking drystone building of huge stones, some weighing two to three tons. (It was probably built in the mid-nineteenth century as a 'Picturesque' cottage that would appeal to the growing tourist trade). The staff offices are situated upstairs but the lower part of the house and the surrounding gardens and four acres of oak woodland are open to the public during the tourist season.

The work of the Society is overseen by the trustees (Executive Committee). Volunteers play a vital part in the Snowdonia Society's work. New members are always welcome whether they wish simply to support the Society's activities and receive the magazine or whether they want to play a more active part in the protection and enhancement of the Snowdonia National Park.

Snowdonia Society, Tŷ Hyll, Capel Curig, Betws-y-coed, North Wales LL24 0DS
Telephone: 01690 720287; E-mail: info@snowdonia-society.org.uk; Web: www.snowdonia-society.org.uk